SORRY ABOUT THE MESS

# SORRY ABOUT THE MESS

*Heather Trickey*

HAPPENSTANCE PRESS

Poems © Heather Trickey, 2020

Cover illustration and graphics © Silva Brindle, 2020

ISBN: 978-1-910131-64-0

Acknowledgements:

Thanks to editors of the following in which some
of these poems, or earlier versions, first appeared
(or are forthcoming): *Quaker Voices, Perverse.*

The 'goose drinking orange juice' graphic on the
inside jacket was first published with
ArtHole Cardiff, 2020.

First published in 2020 by Happen*Stance* Press
21 Hatton Green, Glenrothes KY7 4SD
https://happenstancepress.com

The right of Heather Trickey to be identified
as author of this work has been asserted in accordance
with the Copyright, Designs & Patent Act, 1988

Printed and bound by Imprint Digital, Exeter
https://digital.imprint.co.uk

# Contents

To Simon, Silva, James, Arthur and Nancy

*More than all the world and space*

# GETHSEMANE

*Father, the time has come. Glorify*
*your Son, that your Son may* ... etcetera,
etcetera...
    —John, 17

I'm going to have to trust that John was wrong.
A mission poet, overworking his
material to suit some Grand Agenda,
losing the ring of truth. Like Mark, Matthew
and Luke, I'd have God face-down in the dirt,
sweating blood and sobbing for an out. Cursing
his lovely, shattered friends and fantasising
some neat, impossible, eleventh-hour save:
the priests can't find the gate, Judas has bottled
at the last (the scan was wrong). I need him
to weep (*my soul is overwhelmed*), scoring
the earth with broken nails. I'd have him bargain—
shout—*Is this really all you want from me?*
I'd make him spit the words *Thy Will Be Done.*

## KISS

I confess, I like to chase lice through their hair,
parting the roots to discover a quivering shimmer of mica,
lurking, concealing a blood-sucking heart.

Oh, shiver and run. There's an art, my eye's in,
opposable finger and thumb configure a kiss,
inch up each sticky strand, skin to the air—

*Yay! Check out that biggie!*
In my hand there's a pinprick of writhing despair.
I flick it away.

Two hours in, two more to go at least.
I was Item 4, some aeons past.

The Chair is a magnificent sadist
or she would release me. Instead she pinches

each bastard point between finger and thumb
while we, numb, decorate Any Other

Business with tiny flowers, and plan a final
lunge for the bourbon creams.

## METAMORPHOSIS

She told us quick.
                         A sharp intake
which may have been me.
She wore a knitted cardigan.
Hands folded in her lap.
My cheeks were wet.

Standing like a sentry by the door,
our case nurse broke her pose
to offer a box of Kleenex—
*Christ, no!* And to be fair
Cardigan-Lady seemed to get it.

Or perhaps to be *un*fair. For I
am now a God of the Underworld
staking my claim: Night from Day,
Wrong from Right, Death from Life,
and something crucial but arbitrary

about Cardigan-Lady, perhaps
her neat hands, or the small way
she inclined towards me, struck
my godlike fancy and I saved her
—named her 'Friend'.

Caused me to say *I'm sorry
this can't be the easiest part of your job.*
Caused me to reach for a hug
(while over-her-shoulder I glared
at Sergeant Foe—*the Evil Bitch*).

And then. Waiting for our taxi
—pacing in the insufficient rain—
I shouted *Fuck!* into the faces
of all the living women coming in.

## TALK TO SOMEONE WHO HAS BEEN THROUGH IT

I have had the foresight
to gather among my friends
several whose partner
died of cancer.
                    However,
as yet I have failed
to achieve a connection with
their Significant Other.

## TURN, TURN...

*Oh, what's the bloody point?*
That's what Kenneth Williams said.
I wasn't a fan.

Nonetheless, that weary closing line,
half-arsed doodle of existential dread

    *tread    tread    tread*
    *tread    tread    tread*

was near enough the nail
for a man too numb to feel
the slam of the mallet on his thumb.

## GEOGRAPHY

Helen, poppy red, walks cool through the flaming centre
because that's what you do when you encounter a fire
because life is better lived face-on, full-throttle, high wire
because those ten thousand boats all still need launching
(or burning) before breakfast.

Helen, navy blue, says: *Keeping going is simple, but it's tough.*
She imparts this wisdom to me when I'm nine fathoms drowned
in snot and self-pity. She hooks in a bunch of stuff: an art-house
lobster-based dystopia, an earthquake and an aquanaut.
*Surface over here, when you're ready.*

Helen, sunny yellow, says—*It's geography. We all need
somebody to schlep the kids to the park or feed the cat
at weekends. Move two streets, you're dead to me!*
With neighbours this fierce, this smart, this funny—
who could ever want friends?

Today I'm winning, wearing
green and cerise together,
dangling cherry earrings
to my chin and—*why not?*—
lipstick, even. I am wielding
a new felt tip and crossing
through my To Dos like no
yesterdays, like I was never
one to sit on a sofa sobbing.

CAREFULLY CONSIDERED LIST OF REASONS TO
SUPPORT MY APPLICATION FOR MEMBERSHIP OF
THE RELIGIOUS SOCIETY OF FRIENDS (QUAKERS)
AFTER MORE THAN TWENTY-FIVE YEARS OF
ATTENDING QUAKER MEETINGS

still here

## RANNOCH, BRIDGE OF GAUR

Me, a clumsy child of forty-four,
still trailing Daddy over his winter moor.
Round each remembered contour,
each grass straw, held tight,
enclosed in ice.

He tacks the tussocks, low skedaddles,
looping the blue light. A light foot, straddled
skipper, scape-shifter, whittled
squint of stippled slate
lacing the snow.

Our usual stumble to the loch's end
and a seasonal refrain. An echo, to append
the settled years.

  more deer

                who

      see us
  and flee      over
         a near    ridge /
                    gone

## MARION

I cupped your hand, a parched fist,
in my hand and you opened
a tentative quarter inch.

You thought you knew my name,
strained for it, then rose
like a young queen

to lace a tender arm through mine.
We waltz to way back when
*you are my sunshine*

the long red carpet of the hall.

## WALKING

*Be patterns, be examples in all countries, places, islands, nations,*
*wherever you come; that your carriage and life may preach among*
*all sorts of people, and to them; then you will come to walk cheerfully*
*over the world, answering that of God in everyone.*
    —George Fox, 1656


1  2  3  4  five
once I caught a Quaker
full of cheer

briefly clear /
and maker or no maker
alive

## CREATION

      Out of three stumbling conversations
and six accumulated facts, I have
created you.

      It seems to be enough. And now I'm
polishing and placing shiny pieces: I am gifting you
my *This-Is-Me.*

      Oh, what fine, worn treasures have I!
Silver-lined with cracks. Feel their weathered edges.
This snapped heart is

      exquisite where I want you and
I want you    not   to   touch   .


               On the cracked back of a plastic chair
               two socks (not a pair)
                         Hang *and* Drip

Here's how to do

depression

    Pay attention
    One day
    (why avoid the cliché)
    the world

falls in
and then

*O hell*

many bloody months of boring struggle

For a while    you feel
you can't        go on
             but then    you do
                        Better out than in, you say
                        Yes, once I felt that way
                        but now it's gone    *I'm well*
                        I'd even say I'm stronger
                        somehow clearer now

             oh bum

I'm doing it
all wrong

# ALL SHALL BE WELL

and
all shall be well
and all shall be all shall be
allshallbe all shall be allshall allshall
oh well oh well allshallbe awful awful awful

oh well oh well allshallbe awful oh bloody hell
allshallbe all shall be allshall allshall
and all shall be all shall be
all shall be
and

## LINES COMPOSED WHILE LOOKING FOR
## THE SELLOTAPE

A bottle no lid, a pack with no ace,
a pen with no nib, a snapped dental brace,
a woggle-less necktie, a key to old locks,
a hook with no eye, three mismatched socks,
a legal wrangle, a note I daren't send,
a wickless candle (held) for forfeited friends,
a spoiled vote, inconceivable art,
a hokey-no-cokey, an ill-timed fart,
a task past its deadline, a wayward dove,
a joke with no punchline, a big red bucket
                              of unrequited love,
a pre-prodigal son, a forgivable sin,
no butter, but guns—and the state that we're in,
a cabal and no contest, a paper no news,
a murder no protest, an in-
    escapable
              web of
        infinitely
              flexible
                    truths


and here, at the base of this teetering heap
is half-a-blasted-mind to garner and sweep
our superfluous wreckage, recklessly chuck
the cracked rubble stack of it up, up, UP ...
Old solder won't hold us, I'm all out of string—
if control is our goal, there's no way we can win.

## FOR GRACE RECEIVED BY OPEN MIC

*Well met, friends!*

Here's you and me
animating threads strung across unseen

    frontiers
    tatting the void and

there
that left-hand gesture
                  when I can't find
             a spiral in the air
                  down
                        to a loose-cupped hand

watch them as they slip
               please

just understand
(the way the body speaks)

    *Is this therapy or Art?*
Whether it helps us to carry or convey
             we co-create a squall
                that runs around
                    and in between
           driving us together
        as we tear ourselves apart

a dream, half-seen
        through fraying edges of each other

## CLATTER

We're tired of the clatter inside my head,
ominous missed clicks, synaptic jitter.
It's really nothing like a broken leg—

a kind analogy you use to tread
carefully, to navigate cognitive triggers—
                        *the clatter inside my head.*

You're skirting my lost future tense, my dread
of being inappropriate, embittered,
                        broken.

                                    Some shred

of self-respect flickers,
        *tired of the clatter*

                                    I *am* my head!
Only a marathon runner could suffer
the clatter as she would a broken leg.

No, love, we must be real—not leave unsaid
terror, or the power of our together.
Face it. Nothing like a broken leg, and
                        *we're so tired.*

# SPIRITUAL EXAMEN

*Oh Lord, you have searched me*
*and you know me.*
　　—Psalm 139

Face to face. Forehead almost
touching my forehead. Lips almost
touching my lips. Eyes almost
my own eyes. She presses her palms
down the whole length of my arms.
These tears minister. They calm.

And quiet. Her thumbs hush
across my brow. Her hand's heels push
through my gut. Her fingers brush
this brittle core. Her touch is warm.
Here I stand. *Hineni.* Here I am,
your patient. She eases a thorn.

## ONE SONG FOR ANOTHER

I am listening to Leonard
while working
and thinking of you

I am smiling while listening
to Leonard working
and thinking of you

I am crying and smiling
while listening to Leonard working
and thinking of you

I'm listening and crying
and smiling
and thinking of you

## ON OPENING THE CURTAINS AT DAY BREAK

[                                              ] I've

drawn a glitter storm of lit dust
in cheerful murmuration
see how the morning
stars our breath—
a dawn-dancing
co-creation

bravo!

# BY NIGHT

*There was a man of the Pharisees, named Nicodemus, a ruler of the Jews: the same came to Jesus by night ....*
        —John, 3

I know why Nicodemus came by night
slipping a billowed cloak
across the blind sight of the sun
to offer his surrender
tentatively.

He has more of a comment than a question.
Fells a straw man. Presses
the absurd from mutable words. Oh poor
clumsy lover. When all day long
you have wanted to kneel.

## NATURE POEM

Poised, pen suspended. Time
for me to turn a crafted line
or two to this week's theme:
*Observing the natural world.*

It strikes me now I haven't seen
a single lousy beast. I mean
I saw them but I didn't really look.
A few seagulls, sky-hurled

over the Severn; the odd rook
(or crow, or blackbird, or soot-
y pigeon); whatever up-ended
our bins last night and mauled

our leavings. Could a dismembered
chicken (or its bones) be rendered
in verse? I'm no Ted Hughes.
A paean to The Cat (here, curled

beside me)—maybe that will do.
She yawns. Alas, the muse refuses.
I won't insist this listless rhyme
sings of a universe unfurled—

D minus. Try harder next time.

## ENCOUNTER

The first thing—a shock—she's tiny.
So that, easing the café door
(a greasy spoon, her choice) my glance
passes right over and I'm dripping
on the threshold, until the owner nears
and I explain.

He raises an eyebrow to indicate
the corner table, where I finally
perceive an agitated lady in a blue plaid
leaping between the salt cellar
and the butter dish, making little dents
in the Formica.

A tap on the shoulder. The owner
hands me a pink copper ear-trumpet—
a sod to fit—but now I can make out
what my date is yelling, which is
*You're late!* Make no mistake,
she's hopping mad.

Awkward, but keen to rectify
a bad beginning (a damp packet of drafts
in my coat pocket), I commence a bluster—

she cuts me dead. One finger, dramatic,
to the ceiling—*Your coffee's cold
and I've been waiting here
for forty years.*

# GLYPTODON

*—Arthur, aged seven, reading an illustrated book of extinct animals*

Did you know the Sea Cow
was as long as this room?
The Giant Beaver, as big as a boat,
as tall as Daddy?

Extinct.
Ten thousand years ago.
Stone Age people.

This is quite a sad book.
I don't agree with these animals going extinct.
I wish the Giant Beaver was still here at least.

Did you know,
human beings didn't actually extinct the Glyptodon?
It got extinct by other animals
like the Giant Tortoise, that knocked it out of its way,
then very likely the Passenger Pigeons
who pecked on it and finished it off.

Some of these went extinct after I was born.
I didn't know the minute when they went.

There could still be Dodos around the world.
There could still be Giant Beavers around the world.
Extinction can't be that strong.

If two survived ...
And then there would be babies
Bigger than a tonne.

Oh, the Baby Dwarf Elephant.
I wish the Baby Dwarf Elephant wasn't dead
though.

## POBBLE

After I leaked hot tears onto the radiotherapy bed
and the nurse said she would have liked to give me a hug
but couldn't, I swung by our local patch of water.

This is the Channel. And I am the Pobble,
recklessly dabbling my toes
having already removed my paper mask.

A friend once sat hereabouts and sang a song to the Severn.
*Brown/blue, two things can be true.* Right now it looks
like sparkling shit. This poem is not about Pobbles
and it will not win prizes.

## ACTION PLAN

*April, 2020*

Decision to cancel (or not)
will be based on
coronavirus prevalence,
infection risk,
assessment of potential
gains from treatment
and on what happens
to staffing levels
and NHS capacity.

It is important
that we acknowledge
how you are feeling.

Many families
in your position
have found creative ways
to make lockdown
like the bucket-list
they're missing.
For example—
could you make yours
more like a holiday
by the sea?

## THE STORY OF A ROSE

An artist told me a story about his daughter.
    He showed the girl a rose
    and asked her if she found it beautiful.

He didn't say much about the rose—its colour,
    or whether the petals were open. I suppose
    this single yellow flower must be mine.

He didn't mention the emerald vase,
    which holds the rose perpendicular on a low
    coffee table beneath an attic skylight.

Nothing about how the slant beam catches
    her tangled strands and casts grassy shadows
    onto the whitewashed boards. You know already

the daughter is clever and brave and kind
    and looks just like my own daughter (although
    I gather he meant her to be younger).

What the girl would have made of a cut rose in a vase
    without being asked directly, no one knows.
    However, she does agree the rose is beautiful.

So then the artist hides the yellow flower
    behind his back. *And now?* he asks. *Is the rose
    still beautiful now?* The girl laughs—

*Of course. A yellow rose is beautiful forever.*
    Her answer allows the artist to pose
    this question: *Is beauty a part of the flower*

*or a part of you?*

Whatever.
    A daughter is clever and brave and kind.
    Beautiful. Even if I cannot see her.

# JULIET SURVIVES

[ ... ] *and, when he shall die,*
*Take him and cut him out in little stars,*
*And he will make the face of heaven so fine*
*That all the world will be in love with night*

—Shakespeare, *Romeo and Juliet*

We'd thought it would help.
So late last night I stood
out front and looked up
briefly—a nod.

No moon, and beyond our wall
that 400-watt streetlamp. All I saw,
a purple pall behind the line of roofs.
It didn't move me.

You have to want it—
The Universe, I mean. And lately,
though I ache
endlessly to escape this slow
churning of myself,
I'm lazy.

No muster
to knock that door.

I lack the heart. Not ill,
exactly. And no,
not lonely. Not ready
to risk being still.

## CLEAR

Though you don't ask me to
I'll place this gift of ice
right here, in the hollow of my hand.
I'll fold four fingers, make a lid
and squeeze.
                I'll squeeze
through frozen hell,
through burning skin,
and my endurance will induce
a style of alchemy. Watch me
turning something into nothing
but clear juice.
                Be clear.
Be clear and understand
I am not doing this for you.

## HOMECOMING

*After Derek Walcott's 'Love After Love'*

Hey! Sit down! Eat! Let's outrun
all claims of sleep to tell our stranger stories.
Pour wine. Break bread. Tell me about your heart.

Take mine. After all, I've almost known you
all this time. You, who were abroad
on adventure, encompassing your part,

taking in, absorbing your own commonwealth
of tears and laughter, dreams and hopes,
feel how they've chilled and warmed us—

Come! Let us feast on our lives.

## About The Author

Heather Trickey lives with her husband and four children (two girls, two boys) in the Vale of Glamorgan, where she swims in the sea, all weathers, early in the morning. One of her daughters, Silva Brindle, currently studying Illustration at Camberwell College of Arts, created all the geese that flew into these pages.

It's an established convention that a poetry collection should draw its title from a poem inside it. One of the unresolved messes encompassed here is the lack of a title poem. Sorry.

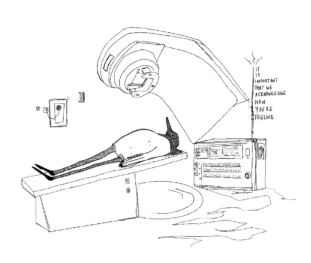

IT
IS
IMPORTANT
THAT WE
ACKNOWLEDGE
HOW
YOU'RE
FEELING